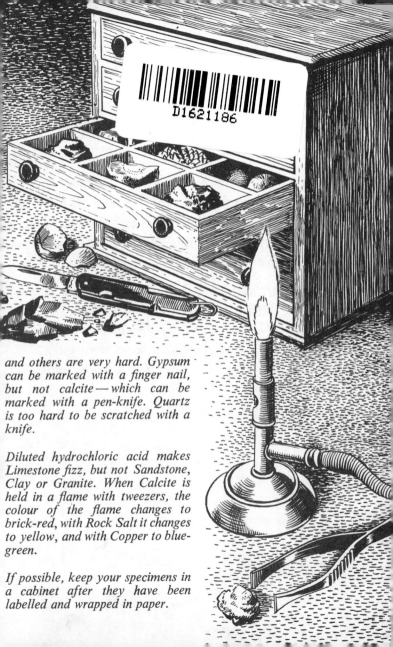

and others are very hard. *Gypsum* can be marked with a finger nail, but not *calcite* — which can be marked with a pen-knife. *Quartz* is too hard to be scratched with a knife.

Diluted hydrochloric acid makes *Limestone* fizz, but not *Sandstone*, *Clay* or *Granite*. When *Calcite* is held in a flame with tweezers, the colour of the flame changes to brick-red, with *Rock Salt* it changes to yellow, and with *Copper* to blue-green.

If possible, keep your specimens in a cabinet after they have been labelled and wrapped in paper.

Series 536

Have you ever realized—as you see or handle a piece of coal—that it is at least two hundred and fifty million years old, or thought of the many other things which we use each day that are just as old—or even older?

Our Earth is full of wonder, and there is much to marvel at under, *as well as on, the surface. This book tells the fascinating story of our rocks and minerals, how they were formed and how they are now used in our daily life.*

THE STORY OF OUR
ROCKS and
MINERALS

by ALLEN WHITE, B.Sc.

with illustrations by ROBERT AYTON

Publishers: Wills & Hepworth Ltd., Loughborough

First published 1966   ©   *Printed in England*

The Nature of the Earth

The Earth is full of wonder. As you look into the sky at night, thousands of stars sparkle like diamonds. All thinking people have asked themselves, "Where did the world come from?" One thing is certain, the earth is part of a large plan, called the Solar System. The sun is at the centre and round it travel the planets, our Earth, Mars, Jupiter, Venus and many others, circling like a giant catherine wheel.

One of the possible explanations of the origin of the Solar System is that a large passing star came close to the sun and pulled out a large part of it, like a giant tooth. This streamed away as a burning gas, and within this flaming gas, spots cooled down changing into the planets.

Over four thousand five hundred million years ago our Earth cooled down into a hot liquid ball, on the outside of which a skin slowly formed. This skin became the crust, with giant mountains and hollows. The rains came, and ran down into the hollows to make the oceans, whilst the higher parts formed the continents.

7214 0106 6

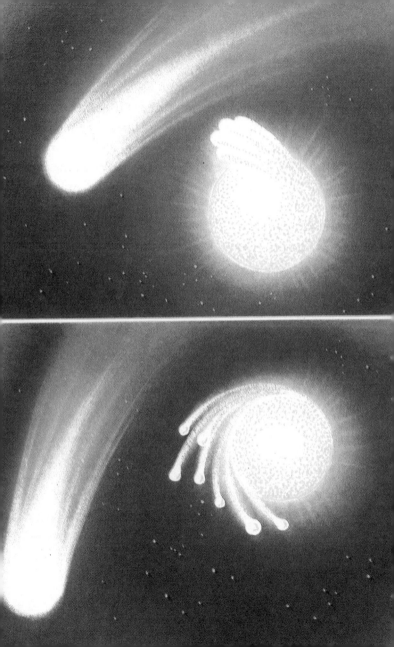

Inside the Earth

Another question everyone asks is, "What would I find if I dug a hole to the centre of the earth?" Some of the deepest coal mines go down three thousand feet, passing through layer after layer of rocks to reach the coal seams. The oil men drill holes more than twenty thousand feet down, but these are only pin-pricks in the earth, which is nearly four thousand miles to the centre.

Beneath the farmers' fields are layers of rocks called strata, many of which contain fossils of animals which lived long ago. These help us to say how old the rocks are. Below the first ten miles the strata begin to disappear and solid granite is found. The continents of the earth are like big rafts of granite floating on a plastic layer called basalt. Sometimes this basalt escapes to the earth's surface and spills out of volcanoes.

Further inwards are heavier spheres of metals, the centre one being the heaviest substance, believed to consist of iron and nickel and extremely hot, as much as four thousand degrees Centigrade. These heavy metals are also found in meteorites which fly around in outer space.

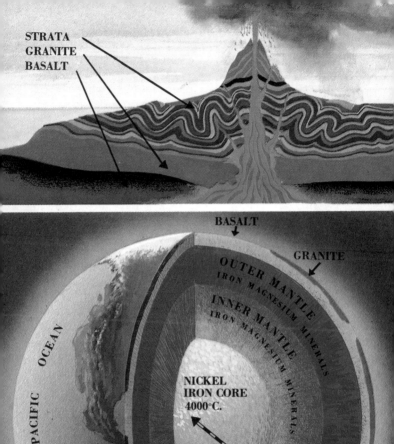

STRATA
GRANITE
BASALT

BASALT

GRANITE

OUTER MANTLE
IRON MAGNESIUM MINERALS

INNER MANTLE
IRON MAGNESIUM MINERALS

PACIFIC OCEAN

NICKEL
IRON CORE
4000°C.

3965 MILES

Earthquakes

Nature has two very violent moods, when earthquakes shake the ground and when volcanoes erupt. These two events are terrifying and destructive for people who live in those parts of the world where they occur, because nothing can be done to stop them.

Recently several big earthquakes have occurred: at Skopje in Yugoslavia in 1963, another in Persia in 1962, and also in Morocco in 1960. These are parts of the world where the rocks are under tremendous strain, and sometimes they break and slide inside the earth. This sudden movement causes vibrations in the earth which make ripples travel along the ground. It is these ripples which topple even the biggest buildings from their foundations.

Sometimes these vibrations start under the sea and gigantic waves rush onto the land, lifting boats out of their harbours and drowning many people. Japan had a disaster in 1923 which caused great fires in Tokyo because it happened at dinner-time. The cooking fires turned over, setting the wooden houses alight and one hundred and fifty thousand people died. Fortunately the British Isles have very firm rock foundations and earthquakes are extremely rare.

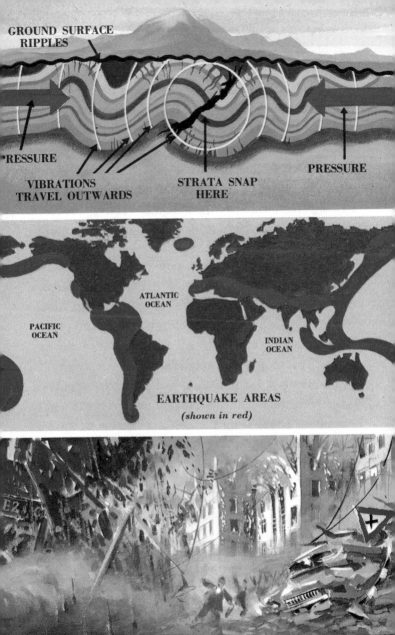

GROUND SURFACE RIPPLES

RESSURE

VIBRATIONS TRAVEL OUTWARDS

STRATA SNAP HERE

PRESSURE

ATLANTIC OCEAN

PACIFIC OCEAN

INDIAN OCEAN

EARTHQUAKE AREAS

(shown in red)

Volcanoes

Volcanic explosions may also set off earthquakes, but these eruptions are more terrifying when they pour out burning lava and shower down hot ashes with suffocating dust clouds. One of the world's biggest volcanic explosions occurred in 1883 on an island, Krakatoa, between Java and Sumatra. This did more damage than the hydrogen bomb. Thirty thousand people were killed and it blew the island off the earth.

Vesuvius, in Italy, is a famous volcano. In A.D. 79 the Romans, living in the city of Pompeii, suffered a disastrous eruption. The exploding mountain buried the city with ash and dust, killing two thousand people. Archaeologists have now uncovered parts of the city again. The people of a tiny island, Tristan da Cunha, in the South Atlantic Ocean, had a similar experience. Their mountain suddenly erupted and everyone had to escape, in boats, from the hot lava flowing down over the island.

Volcanoes occur where the Earth's crust is weakest, and eruptions start deep down. Here the rocks are very hot and under great pressure. Sometimes the pressure builds up until it blows a hole through to the surface, and up this chimney flows the lava.

Rocks from the sea

The rivers of the world are constantly taking tiny particles off the land and spreading this sediment over the sea floor, where it builds up layer upon layer, forming 'sedimentary rocks' such as sandstone and clay. Big rivers like the Thames and Rhine carry millions of tons of mud into the sea. The Mississippi river takes twenty-four thousand tons of chemicals and over one million tons of mud into the Gulf of Mexico each day.

We make many things from these sedimentary rocks. Bricks are made from clay rocks, as are plates, cups, saucers, roof-tiles and drain pipes. We are able to reach this clay because the sea has sometimes changed its position, and these rocks have become dry land.

Limestone and chalk are also sedimentary rocks, being formed over millions of years by the shells of dead sea creatures which sank to the sea bed. Fossil creatures such as ammonites (coil shells) found in limestone prove that the strata were once beneath the ocean. Limestone was used to build the Houses of Parliament, and in the Pennines the rock is burned to make cement and builders' lime.

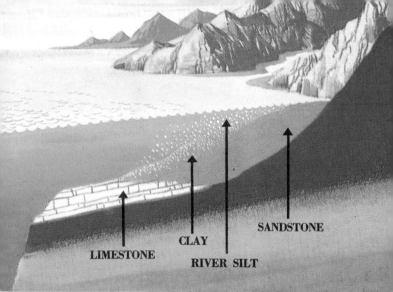

LIMESTONE

CLAY

RIVER SILT

SANDSTONE

Fossils of sea creatures

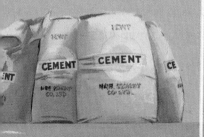

CEMENT *from Limestone*

CEMENT
CEMENT

POTTERY *from Clay*

A Rock Garden in the sea

Just as—millions of years ago—the limestone rocks were formed from the shells of tiny living creatures, so to-day is the Coral Barrier Reef of Australia being formed by life in the ocean. This reef is made of millions of tiny animals, called polyps, growing in the warm shallow waters of coral seas. The reef is like a beautiful underwater garden with sea anemones, tiny bushlike branching corals, mushroom-like fungi and others—all brightly coloured and spreading fine tentacles into the sea, extracting food for their life and lime for their hard shells. When they die, their shells remain and are pressed together to form rock.

Three-quarters of the earth's surface is now made up of sedimentary strata which were once beneath the sea.

In some areas the clay rocks contain gypsum and salt. Gypsum makes plaster of Paris (used for helping to mend broken limbs), and rock salt makes hydrochloric acid, chlorine for purifying swimming baths and table salt for food.

Above—*Corals at low tide*   Below—*Sea anemones*

Stalactites, Stalagmites and Mineral Veins

Most of the rock in the Pennine Hills is mountain limestone—formed under the sea two hundred and fifty million years ago. This limestone contains large cracks into which rain soaks away, and sometimes whole rivers disappear underground. Potholers enjoy exploring the underground passages and caverns.

The Mendip Hills are made of the same kind of rock. At Cheddar the caverns are very large, and here can be found giant stalactites and stalagmites. These have been formed over millions of years by the constant dripping of water from the roofs of the caves. Each drop of water leaves a tiny crystal of lime on the roof, and gradually a long stone icicle—a stalactite—is formed. Each drop falling on the floor leaves another crystal there, and so builds upwards to make a stalagmite.

Crystals formed in this way sometimes fill up cracks in the rocks, when they are known as veins or lodes. Other minerals are produced by great heat and pressures deep in the earth; diamonds form this way. Some minerals are brought up from within the earth by very hot liquids; lead is formed in this way when the hot liquid cools and results in a mineral vein.

Mr. Herbert P. Hugh

Lead

Among the wonders of the Ancient World were the Hanging Gardens of Babylon. Built on pillars three hundred feet high, these terrace gardens had flower beds lined with lead to hold water. This was one of the earliest uses for lead.

The Romans also were expert builders and many of their camps had baths fitted with lead pipes. At Bath, these pipes are still in use after two thousand years. When the Romans lived in Britain they searched the hills for galena, the commonest lead ore, which they found as grey cubes in the limestone rocks. The Romans called it 'plumbum' and so a plumber was someone who fixed water-pipes.

Galena is now melted in furnaces and treated so that the hot lead runs into moulds where it sets. Because it never rusts, it was often used on the roofs of churches, but now it is too expensive. Nearly one-third of all lead used to-day goes into batteries, as every motor car must have one. Telephone cables under the sea are lead covered. Paint contains lead and so do the 'sinkers' (boots) used by divers.

18

THE HANGING GARDENS OF BABYLON

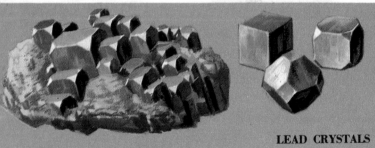

LEAD CRYSTALS

Iron Ore and Steel

Lodestone is Nature's magnetic iron ore (Magnetite), and the first compass used by sailors was a floating needle of lodestone. Iron ore is a very important mineral, as many things like bicycles, cars, trains, gas-stoves and tools start as ore in the earth. Pyrites, siderite and hematite are the commonest ironstones, the last being the most important.

The making of steel begins when machines dig out the ironstone rocks. In the blast furnace this ore is melted at two thousand degrees Centigrade, together with coke and limestone. White hot liquid iron is run off, through the tapping hole, every four hours. This 'pig' iron is then taken either to the 'Bessemer' or Open-hearth furnaces to be made pure. A mixture of ninety-nine parts pure iron and one part carbon makes steel, but for special steels manganese or tungsten are also added.

Ingots of white hot steel are then rolled and squeezed into shapes like girders, railway lines or flat sheets. These, later, form parts of bridges, railway tracks, ships or tin-plate. We handle tin-plate every day when we open tins of food.

IRON ORE

Opencast working

Pouring off
Steel Ingots

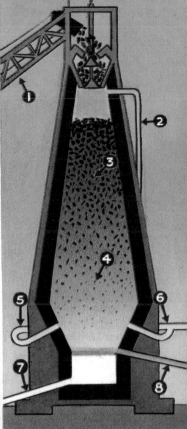

BLAST FURNACE

1. Hopper feed of iron ore, coke and limestone.
2. Escape of hot gases.
3. Iron ore, coke and limestone.
4. 2000° C.
5 and 6. Hot air blasts.
7. Molten iron.
8. Flow off of slag.

Quartz, Agate and Glass

Quartz is one of the commonest minerals found in the earth. Perfect crystals are sometimes found in granite rocks, but they are very rare. They are six-sided (hexagonal) with pointed ends, often as clear as glass—which is why we say 'clear as crystal'. The ancient Greeks called it 'krystallos', meaning 'clear ice'.

Some coloured crystals are shaped into gems, amethyst is purple quartz, and citrine is golden yellow quartz. Agate is a special form which is easily known by its many coloured stripes.

Quartz has many important uses. Sand is a form of quartz which is mixed with cement for building houses and factories; pure white sand is necessary for making glass. Glass sand must be free of iron so that it melts in the furnace into clear glass, which can be shaped by the glass-blower. In the glass factories window glass, jam jars and many glass ornaments are made. Crystal quartz is very useful in radio stations and radar instruments. Pure radio quartz controls the radio waves, but it is very scarce. Scientific lenses and dishes, which must resist acids, are also made from quartz.

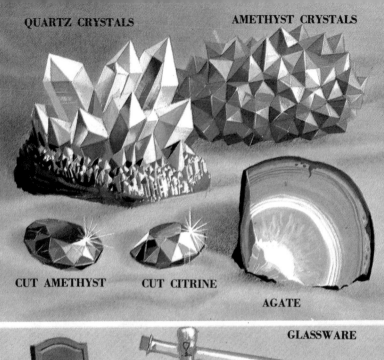

QUARTZ CRYSTALS

AMETHYST CRYSTALS

CUT AMETHYST

CUT CITRINE

AGATE

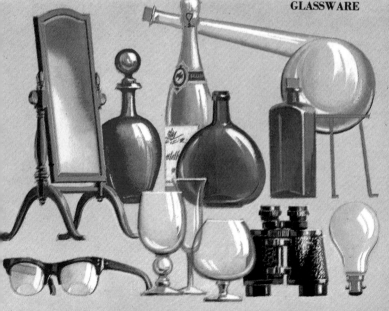

GLASSWARE

Graphite

Writing is easy with a piece of graphite because it is a soft stone which makes black marks on paper, as well as soiling the fingers. The ancient Greeks, who used this black stone, called it 'graphite', meaning 'writing'.

Graphite has often been mistaken for lead because it has the same colour, and this is why we speak of 'lead' pencils which are not really lead at all. The thin lead in a pencil is made by mixing graphite powder with clay and heating it in a furnace to over one thousand five hundred degrees Centigrade, Soft leads have more graphite than hard ones. Nearly one-tenth of all graphite mined is used in pencils, but its chief use is for making special cups and basins in which to melt brass and other metals. Dynamo 'brushes' are also made of graphite.

Sometimes oil cannot be used on machines in cloth factories as it might run and mark the material, so powdered graphite is used instead. Atomic power stations use a lot of graphite because an atomic reactor is made by placing rods of uranium in huge blocks of graphite.

GRAPHITE

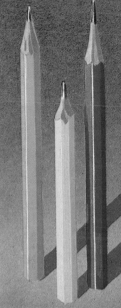

Pencils

Atomic Power Station

Dynamo brushes

Crucible for melting
precious metals

Sulphur

When Guy Fawkes tried to blow up the Houses of Parliament he used the only explosive then known— gunpowder. Sulphur is part of the recipe for making gunpowder and although modern explosives do not use gunpowder, it forms part of the fireworks we buy for November 5th.

Sulphur is sometimes called 'brimstone' or 'burn-stone', as it is one of the few minerals which melt easily and catch fire. It burns with a terrible smell and choking fumes, just as a volcano does when it erupts. Burning volcanoes, geysers and hot springs give out sulphur fumes, and in New Zealand and Iceland the caves are often lined with lovely yellow sulphur crystals.

Sulphuric acid is the most important product made from sulphur. Large quantities of this acid are used in the manufacture of fertilizers for agriculture, in the making of paint, and in the production of paper and rayon from wood pulp. Natural rubber is too soft for motor tyres, but when sulphur is mixed with it the rubber becomes very hard and tough. This is called 'vulcanized' rubber.

SULPHUR CRYSTALS

Fluorspar and Blue John

Fluorspar is not a very common mineral in the British Isles. It is mined in only two counties, Derbyshire and Durham. The word 'fluor' means 'to flow' and this describes the main use of fluorspar in purifying steel, silver and gold. For every ton of steel in the furnace, ten pounds of fluorspar are added to make the waste products 'flow off' as a scum on the molten steel. In this way, the purified metal is left behind to set in ingots.

The second main use for this mineral is in the pottery industry. It is one of the substances used to make the enamel on the baths and kitchen sinks in our homes.

Natural crystals are found in the limestone rocks of Derbyshire and Durham, and are shaped in cubes, yellow, brown, green or pink, and more rarely blue, when it is called 'Blue John'. Many of our cathedrals have beautiful stained glass windows, some of which were coloured by mixing fluorspar in the glass.

A modern use for fluorspar is in the making of fluoride toothpaste, said to strengthen teeth.

BLUE JOHN CAVERNS

FLUORSPAR BLUE JOHN

FLUORSPAR GREEN

Granulated Fluorspar being fed into steel making furnace

...ear as glass, but when you look ...it is a magic mineral. Everything ..., and words are blurred because ...tten twice, closely, side by side. ...e letters slowly join together and ...his is called 'double-refraction'. The best crystals come from Iceland, and are known as 'Iceland-spar'.

This mineral is used inside the special microscopes which geologists use to look into rocks. Experts testing diamonds, emeralds and other gemstones use special instruments containing Iceland-spar lenses to find out if the gems are genuine.

Impure calcite is a very common mineral found in all limestone hills like the Pennines and the Cotswolds. As we have seen on an earlier page, the stalactites and stalagmites which are found in the caverns of these hills are made of millions of tiny crystals of calcite, formed from the lime in the water which trickles through the rocks.

Rainwater slowly dissolves limestone and passes on into rivers, making the water 'hard'. This causes kettles to 'fur-up' with hard stony lumps, and the water-pipes in our homes to become blocked with a crust of lime.

CALCITE CRYSTALS

Lime deposit shown in kettle and water pipe.

Rock Salt

It is impossible to sink in the Dead Sea because it contains so much salt. The river Jordan brings in the salt and the hot sun evaporates the water from the sea, leaving the salt behind.

The salt layers in the rocks in Cheshire were formed millions of years ago when seas and lakes dried up. Now miners work four-hundred feet underground in big caverns, taking out rock salt which is made pure in the factory on the surface.

Salt is a vital part of our daily lives, we all eat about twelve pounds every year. It is put into the cooking, and food is sometimes stored in salt. Animals need salt, so the farmer buys 'salt-lick' for his cows. Chemicals are made from salt, soda being one of the most important as it is used in glass-works, and in soap and paper making. Chlorine, from salt, purifies water and makes acid as well as cleansing powders. Salt melts ice on the door-steps of our homes, and nowadays large quantities are mixed with sand to help roadmen to clear snow from the roads.

ROCK SALT

Crystals

Salt mining

China-clay

Near St. Austell, in Cornwall, large white mounds can be clearly seen on the hillsides. These are china-clay workings, and this soft white clay is a very special mineral. It is called 'kaolin', a Chinese name for some hills in that country from which pottery clay has been obtained for many centuries. Two-hundred years ago we bought clay from China, but now we find enough in Cornwall and Devon. Large patches of kaolin are found in the granite rocks, where strong gases have attacked the crystals and caused the rocks to crumble. Here the miners wash out the soft clay with powerful jets of water.

Large quantities of china-clay are sent to the factories at Stoke-on-Trent to be made into cups, saucers, plates and all kinds of pottery. Another use for this pure clay is in the manufacture of certain kinds of paper: these papers have a smooth, glossy surface necessary for some methods of printing.

Kaolin is also used in the manufacture of rubber, paint, linoleum, soap, facepowders, stomach powders and poultices.

CHINA CLAY WORKINGS

Asbestos

Asbestos looks more like a plant than a mineral from the earth. It is nature's 'rock-wool' because it is made of soft silky fibres, which can be easily pulled apart. These fibres are not affected by intense heat, strong acid or electricity and will never rot away. This makes it a very special substance, useful for many purposes.

The Romans knew about this everlasting mineral and used it for lamp-wicks. The first fireproof coat was made from asbestos one hundred and fifty years ago, and to-day it is used for firemen's clothes, helmets and escape ropes.

The fibres of asbestos are spun and woven into cloth, just like cotton and wool, for making special clothes and curtains. A well-known use is for safety-curtains in cinemas and theatres. In older theatres the safety curtains still have 'ASBESTOS' written on them. Modern houses have asbestos water-tanks in the roofs as these will never go rusty or leak like metal ones. All cars, buses and lorries use asbestos in the brake-linings, because it never gets too hot or melts when the brakes are used.

ASBESTOS

Motor brake lining

SAFETY
CURTAIN

Coal

Every time you put a lump of coal on the fire, you are using something nearly two-hundred and fifty million years old. It began in the huge swamps which covered some parts of Britain, and in which plants and trees grew in thick jungles. The trees were different from those of to-day because they had soft trunks or hollow stems, like giant mosses, huge ferns or horsetail trees. In the warm swamps these plants grew, rotted away and were replaced by others, so that great thicknesses of dead plants piled up on top of one another.

The bottom of the swamps continually sank, and sometimes water completely covered the forests. When this happened, rivers brought in tons of mud and covered all the swamp plants with layers of rock. In this way the forests were squashed into coal seams. Two-hundred feet of rotting plants made a coal seam ten feet thick. Above these seams and rocks, swamp forests grew again, later to be submerged in turn. This went on for millions of years, gradually forming the coal seams of to-day.

FOSSIL PLANTS IN COAL

COALFACE

COAL SEAMS BETWEEN
LAYERS OF ROCK STRATA

Mining and using our coal

A modern coal mine is like the underground railway in London, but very much deeper. Bradford Colliery, near Manchester, goes down over three thousand feet. Every day many miners go down the main shaft, each one carrying a lamp on his helmet.

Special electric or diesel trains take the men several miles to their work at the coal face. In the older pits the miners have a hard task breaking the coal and loading the wagons. The modern mines have powerful machines which rip out the coal and load it on to conveyor belts to start its journey to the surface. Powerful railway engines, pulling one hundred tons of coal, make many journeys to the main shaft. Here it is like a railway station complete with signals, fluorescent lighting and automatic telephones.

Coal has many uses other than for fires. Gasworks use coal to make gas, and at the same time produce chemicals for dyes, paints, soap and many other things. Iron and steel works use many tons of coke every day, and electricity is made at some power stations by burning coal dust.

Every year our mines produce two hundred million tons of coal. This would fill a coal train fifty thousand miles long and stretching twice round the world.

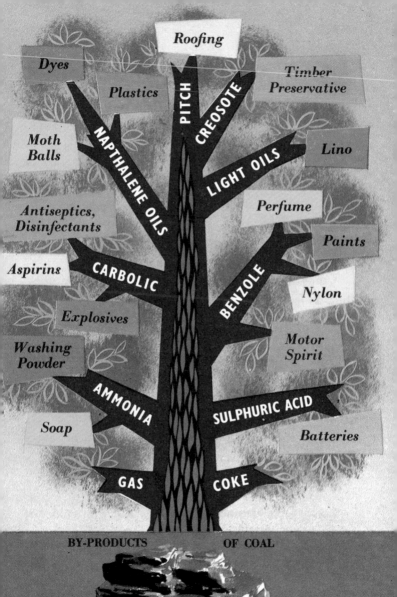

Roofing

Dyes

Timber
Preservative

Plastics

PITCH

CREOSOTE

Moth
Balls

NAPTHALENE OILS

Lino

LIGHT OILS

Antiseptics,
Disinfectants

Perfume

Paints

Aspirins

CARBOLIC

BENZOLE

Nylon

Explosives

Washing
Powder

Motor
Spirit

AMMONIA

SULPHURIC ACID

Soap

Batteries

GAS

COKE

BY-PRODUCTS   OF COAL

Silver

Silver has been used since 4,000 B.C. to make fine ornaments and jewellery. Many were discovered in the ancient tombs of the Kings of Persia and Mesopotamia.

The Spaniards were looking for silver in Peru and Mexico when they explored South America, and there they discovered nuggets weighing nearly a ton. The Spanish galleons were real treasure ships carrying the precious metal back to the King of Spain.

Coins have been made from silver for many centuries, but, as it is very soft, it has to be mixed (alloyed) with copper and nickel to make it hard.

Special chemicals which are very sensitive to light, are made from silver. This is the secret of taking photographs with a camera or films for the cinema or television. The reel in the camera contains these very sensitive chemicals. We all look into the mirror every day, yet it is the silvered back of the glass which really reflects.

Some silver is mined out of the earth with gold, but most of this metal is found mixed with lead and copper ores in Bolivia, Mexico and Peru.

HALL MARK ON SILVER

MAKERS INITIALS		STERLING QUALITY	
	MADE IN SHEFFIELD		DATE MARK

SILVER ORE

Gold

In the days of Pharaoh, three thousand years ago, the Egyptians were using gold to make beautiful cups, bowls and necklaces. These are still as perfect as when they were first made. Gold is the 'King of metals' because it never loses its bright colour or decays away. This is why it has been used for centuries as money. The Mint in London is the place where coins have long been made from bars of solid gold.

Gold leaf is made by beating it into thin sheets, and this is possible because it is a very soft metal. Usually it is hardened by being mixed with copper or silver. The purity of gold is measured in 'carats': twenty-four carat is pure gold, which is too soft for use. Fourteen carat is the usual strength for pen nibs. Wedding rings are twenty-two carat. The dentist sometimes uses gold for filling teeth, and gold paint is used for patterns on cups and saucers.

Gold is found in rivers by sifting the sand in large pans and, when finds are made, the miners search the hills for the mineral veins of gold. One famous nugget found in Australia was worth ten-thousand pounds.

GOLD NUGGET

GOLD FLAKE IN QUARTZ

Gold Panning

3000 year old Gold Mask of King Tut-ankh-amen

Oil and Petrol

'Noah's Ark' and 'Moses in the Bulrushes' are stories which are linked with oil. The ark and the Moses basket were made waterproof with pitch, which formed long ago from an oil leak in the earth.

Mineral oil is found in certain rocks, which were formed millions of years ago beneath the sea. Countless tiny animals, once living in the oceans, sank into the muds on the sea floor and changed into specks of oil. Other deposits followed and formed into rocks. A long time afterwards, gigantic forces within the earth raised these rocks from the sea bed to form new land, and often rock-arches were created. Into the crests of the arches, oil was squeezed and trapped.

Boring a hole into the rocks takes a long time and costs over three hundred thousand pounds. The crude oil from the borehole is a mixture of many kinds. One part may be suitable for jet aeroplanes, another for cars, some for diesel engines, whilst the bitumen (pitch) is used on the roads. The refinery splits oil into its different qualities, and some help to make rubber, linoleum, waxed containers, plastics, perfumes, medicine, disinfectants, etc.

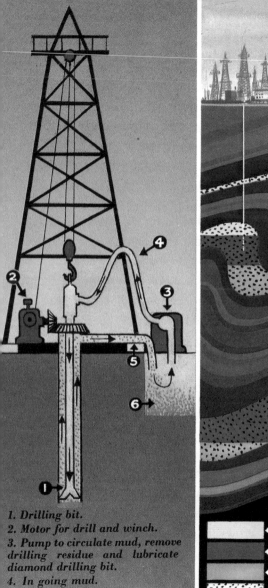

1. Drilling bit.
2. Motor for drill and winch.
3. Pump to circulate mud, remove drilling residue and lubricate diamond drilling bit.
4. In going mud.
5. Out going residue.
6. Mud reservoir.

Gas
Oil
Water
Porous Rock
Impervious Rock

Diamonds and Pearls

The earth sometimes yields rare and priceless gems. King of all gemstones is the diamond. This is the hardest mineral on earth, and impure diamonds are very useful for cutting steel, making grinding or polishing wheels, rocks drills, and diamond-tipped needles for record-players.

The Crown Jewels in the Tower of London contain the world's finest diamonds. The Royal Sceptre has the largest of all, the First Star of Africa, flashing its emblem of Justice and Kingship. The Imperial State Crown, used at Coronations, has the Second Star of Africa. These came from the largest stone ever found in South Africa, the Cullinan Diamond.

A diamond is a simple substance because it is pure carbon, but it has been made into a crystal by great heat and pressure inside the earth and brought to the surface by ancient volcanoes.

Pearls are gems from the sea, formed in some oyster shells when sand irritates the animal inside the shell. The animal covers the sand grain with mother of pearl and the pearl grows bigger each year. Divers find pearl-oysters in the Red Sea and Indian Ocean.

Natural rock with diamond embedded

Above
*The Imperial Sceptre
with the magnificent
Cullinan diamond, its
actual size is 2¼″ deep.*

Left
*The Imperial State
Crown with the second
Cullinan diamond.*

PEARLS

Radioactive Minerals

Ours is the Atomic Age. It began when Professor and Madame Curie discovered radium in 1898. Professor Curie found that radium gave out invisible rays which could pass through many things and he called this power 'radioactivity'. These rays have special powers useful for combating some illnesses.

Some of the earth's minerals show this radioactive power very strongly. Pitchblende is the best known because it contains radium and uranium. In 1939 scientists succeeded in bursting uranium atoms and releasing great power, and this discovery resulted in the atomic bombs which destroyed two Japanese cities in 1945.

The most helpful ways of using this new power are in power stations and ships. In 1958 the famous atomic submarine, *Nautilus,* sailed under the ice-pack which surrounds the North Pole. The atomic reactor in the engine helped to keep the ship moving, and it travelled for ninety-six hours beneath the ice.

In atomic power stations, heat is created by splitting millions of uranium atoms every second in a reactor. This heat is used to produce steam which drives the turbines. These in turn drive the electric generators.

Radioactive
PITCHBLENDE

Nuclear Power Station

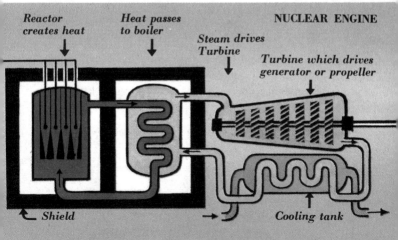

NUCLEAR ENGINE

Reactor creates heat

Heat passes to boiler

Steam drives Turbine

Turbine which drives generator or propeller

Shield

Cooling tank

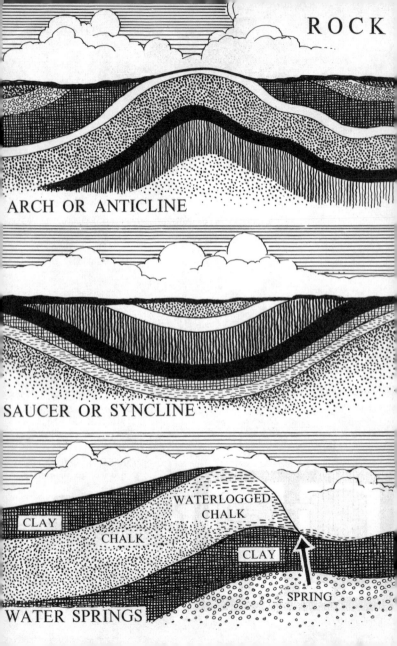

ROCK

ARCH OR ANTICLINE

SAUCER OR SYNCLINE

CLAY

WATERLOGGED CHALK

CHALK

CLAY

SPRING

WATER SPRINGS